Moving Beyond

--- ∞ ---

*Musings on
Solitude, Awareness,
and Manifestation*

JMG

Moving Beyond: Musings on Solitude, Awareness, and Manifestation

© 2023, JMG
jmg@hipcity.co
Hip City Inc.

ISBN: 978-1-7355593-3-9

Cover and interior design by Tabitha Lahr

All rights reserved. No part of this publication may be reproduced, stored in a retrieval system, stored in a database and / or published in any form or by any means, electronic, mechanical, photocopying, recording or otherwise, without the prior written permission of the publisher. If you enjoyed this book, please encourage your friends to download their own copy from their favorite authorized retailer. Thank you for your support.

Printed in the United States of America

Moving Beyond

To EB and M Sol

Accept Solitude 1

Develop Awareness 29

Play with Manifestation 59

Accept Solitude

"Then stirs the feeling infinite, so felt in solitude,
where we are least alone."

New steps...

on the horizon. Settle in and look for the path in stillness. Slowly become aware of what surrounds you. A world that comes to you without an agenda. Opening your mind to possibilities and pathways. No one step greater than the other, just forward progress by the moment. Lean in to the sights and sounds of peaceful resolution. Allow what will happen to happen without judgment or worry. Trust that all is working in your favor, and it will be.

Why . . .

do so many seem to be looking for an instant result? What is wrong with letting things settle for a bit and watching them work themselves out? Instant gratification erodes your true being. You will begin to obsess over the little things and miss the big picture. We are designed to be visionaries, not simple categories to be filed away. If you let yourself be caught up in the minutia, you will never be happy. It is only after you step away and breathe can you let the elements coalesce.

Sometimes . . .

you find yourself in an environment that stifles. The energy is stagnant, and the pace has halted. What lies ahead seems bottlenecked and blocked. When you find yourself in this situation, go ahead and physically remove yourself from the surroundings. You may experience some discomfort while you do this, but it is worth the change of scenery. Once you're back on stable footing, you will be rewarded. Your energy will rise, and your rhythm will stabilize. But you will not know this until you make the choice to find out.

Don't force . . .

the issue. Know when to rest and recharge. Nobody is chasing you. This is your path to take. Flow with the energy provided. Check in daily. If something feels misaligned, pause and ask what if. . . . Be kind to yourself as you plot your next move. Remember, there is no specific timetable, and all is happening around you as it should.

It's OK...

to take your time. Let things marinate as they will. But keep focusing on what you want to have happen. Or you think you want to have happen. The gears keep turning, even while you sleep. Accept what comes when it comes, and long for nothing. It will be here soon enough. Take each day as it comes and appreciate all you have been given to succeed. Remember, what you focus on expands. It is your choice, after all, so choose what brings you and your family the most joy and freedom. Let the chatter be.

You can . . .

hold on to only so much. Learn to release and let go of the unproductive stories weighing on your mind. Realize they're an illusion or a program that your mind is running on your behalf. It affects you only if you believe it. If the matter did really concern you, it would be solved already. So drill down to the essence of things and let go. Once you do, you have space for the productive stories. The ones that can open your world up, not close it down. Trust that the best is yet to come, and it will start to appear.

You are beginning . . .

to wake up. You know this because you feel uneasy about your environment. Everything you thought you knew has been turned upside down. It all seems different. And yet the same. You are now becoming aware of ideas on a grand scale. This might be disconcerting, but it does not have to be. It can be an opportunity to begin to understand the vastness that lurks underneath. Don't wish for things to get back to normal, because that was an illusion in the first place. There is no "normal". Once you're awake, there is no going back. There are only more and more realizations on how far you are going.

When you . . .

live in the moment, time has no meaning. It acts like a mirage, triggering feelings one moment to the next. But you can't place it. Because it's fleeting and stagnant. And you are OK with all of it. It seems to expand and compress. Bend and disappear in an instant. The feeling of being gone for a day can seem like a year. In the end the sun comes up and you have another chance. All you can build on is each day. When you live in each moment fully, the future will take care of itself.

There is . . .

nowhere to go. There is everywhere to go. A connection, a garden, a voice in the wilderness. A shadow that sticks by you, and lungs that breathe in and out. As everyone begins to find their footing, we will venture out. Into the unknown, into the abyss, and into our soul's progression. The choice is yours on how you want to live. In exile or in celebration? In fear or in possibility? In scarcity or abundance? In the predictions or in the now? Keep asking these questions over and over. Be patiently attentive to the answers.

Once you . . .

allow yourself freedom and autonomy, there is no going back to how things were. Even if you did, you would not recognize it. All we do is adapt little by little and day by day. To accept this is an easeful flow state; to deny this is disjointed frustration. When you realize this, all that happens, happens for your purpose of being. Life is simple. We just tend to imagine it's not. Many inputs we receive are telling us we are not enough, but that is all noise. Don't let them entangle you.

Find your . . .

resources of energy at your disposal. Don't grasp. There is no rush; you only think there is—create to create and leave the rest alone. Begin to eliminate things that don't serve you, which will make more space for things that do. Be mindful in the examination. Take notice of what brings you joy. From this place everything flows. Stagnation does not take shape, for it has no place to. You move lightly and effortlessly from one station to the next. Collecting resources and making discoveries along the way.

All separation . . .

is false. It is created by the mind and is temporary and fleeting. It is created as an idea to keep you safe, but it eventually does the opposite. You are so boxed in to one way of thinking that all other avenues become closed. The rigid structure gets tighter and tighter until it snaps. Reality will always re-assert itself. You are presented a choice: to live in the past, future, or entirely in the now. Be aware of your surroundings and proceed with minimal interference. In the end, what you are you can never know, but what you are not, you can.

Go through . . .

shedding. Of old patterns, of old beliefs, of old paradigms. You'll feel uneasy. You will feel stuck. You will turn inward for protection. The world will confuse you. It's OK. It's the natural way to shed. Your mind will cling to what's familiar. But it's changing, because changing is in its DNA. There is a new evolution occurring. People around you won't see it yet. They will feel your discomfort. Just stay the course. You will break through into the other side.

Develop Awareness

"The key to growth is the introduction of higher dimensions of consciousness into our awareness."

There is . . .

no more waiting. The cosmic leaps are here and now. You have felt them brewing and seeping into your awareness. There is no more striving, there is just doing. Embrace the process of discovery, and life becomes what you crave without grasping for anything. You let the hooks straighten so there is nothing to hold you stagnant or to get stuck on. If you look around, you will start to notice all the cracks in the foundation of what are perceived as monolithic structures. Things you grew up with which held a strong seat at the table are being exposed for the paper tigers they are. Once you get over the shock and discomfort, you can begin to see the significance of it. Everything is now on the table. It always has been, but more and more people are becoming aware of it. Where it leads is an opportunity to create our day-to-day existence. There is nothing to be afraid of. We are built to adapt, to change, and to thrive.

How to . . .

create what you want to see. First, let go of the *how*. Let your mind dream up creative ways to see it. It's all there to access; you just have to make the connection to do so. The building blocks are all out on the table. Keep practicing awareness to harness them. Don't bend and twist, just allow it to happen. When you do this you become part of the whole. You begin to realize what has been there all along for you to participate in or not pay attention to.

Accept . . .

each moment as it is and have full awareness that it will pass. It may be what you perceive as good or bad, painful or joyful, but rest assured, all of it changes. Rejoice in this and use it to your advantage. Great power can come from this, as you can detach from worrying if it will come back around to joy. It always does.

A truth . . .

exists in an interpretation of past events as seen through our eyes. What we think of as truths are thoughts after the fact to justify or to understand why something has happened. But there is no logical reason why some things go one way and other things go another way. What we do have at our disposal is awareness of the passing moment. We have awareness of our feelings and of the opportunity being offered. We have awareness of our surroundings. We can choose to run toward whatever we're aware of, or run away from it.

Recognize . . .

that the collective consciousness around you moves in waves. It will ebb and flow. It is never an absolute. Changes arrive in fits and starts. Something can seem so concrete, but will vanish the next day. Other times a seemingly empty space is filled overnight. The important thing is to remain a witness to it. This way you do not attach yourself to it. When you are able to do this, the events lose power over you. Life becomes playful and full of amazing observations and opportunities that are malleable. In pursuing your truth, you will find out what is false.

It's time . . .

to move beyond. Beyond the back and forth. Beyond the day to day. Beyond the true and false. Beyond the past and future. Beyond the fear and safety. Beyond the virtue and deceit. Beyond the causation and pattern recognition. Beyond the particles you think you are, and into the energy of being. Into a place of awareness, gratitude, and acceptance.

The glass ceiling . . .

is being shattered. As we gain more and more awareness, we will start to see lasting changes. Disregard the illusions that will proliferate in your mind, preventing momentum. Move forward. There is nothing to fight per se. It's more like re-direct. For it is not a zero-sum game. This life is about letting go and filtering your reality to help yourself and others. We are all figuring it out. Slowly but surely.

Create . . .

to uncover and to explore. To focus in on being and to focus in on awareness. Ride the waves up and down, and the tides that pull back and forth. The walls are there for you to see but not buy into. The old paradigm of exclusion is falling away. There is no need to escape because the access is here and now. We are all a part of it. Even if we don't realize it. It is a great reset. And we have a chance to participate and build on it.

You can't be . . .

in growth mode and protection mode at the same time. This is because protection will override growth. Ask yourself, is the defense worth the sacrifice to growth? Or do you want the environmental factors of growth to be nurtured and set up for success? Awareness is the key. Are you fulfilled by being in protection mode? Then do so and don't apologize for it. Accept the consequences until you realize you would like to go a different way. You will know when you know. Then shift your mindset to the possibilities of growth, and all sorts of things will be open for you to explore. Go easy on yourself; life is supposed to fun.

The days . . .

of retreating or numbing ourselves into complacency are over. We must face our truth. With awareness of the moment, we can start listening to this. Opting out is no longer an option. We are all in this together. Separation does not exist. Move into a space where your mind works for your soul's desire, not against it. Embrace your connection with the environment. Honor the power of your own mind when it comes to resilience and anti-fragility. Take each day as it comes. Take deep breaths and be grateful. Understand your opportunity for expansion. Undertake what lies in front of you. Do what feels best. If something is not flowing, stop and readdress. Pay attention to the wind.

How . . .

to accept it all and none. How to embrace the natural flow of things and how to open chains of salvation and rebirth. What if you just embrace it? The fluid movement of unexpected discovery and joy. The recommitment of thoughts and gratitude. The nocturnal awareness from beyond and back again. The facts colliding in a sea of misinformation and judgment. The escape through screens in order to fulfill your purpose to the outside. The inside twirling away, finding new passages and new space to venture. The comfort zone no longer holding water. The fissures have become gaps in reality and consciousness. The ramblings of a new rising and the unfolding of habits and circles never end. We are all on the same path but imagine we're not, until we meet at the signpost.

We are all . . .

marching on day by day and hour by hour. The old world is crumbling. The labels, the definitions, the explanations all do not make sense any longer. We are evolving, and many are scared. But you don't have to be. You can be in the flow of the current just as easily as against it. You can let it work for you just as much as it seems to work against you. The institutions that propped up this old world are being transformed or going away. The new way is around the corner; you just can't see it yet. But you can feel it. You can feel the angst, the desire, the longing for control. But we don't have control and we never did. There was always an illusion of it, nothing more. What is in your control and the only thing that really is, is awareness in the moment. Awareness of how you are reacting. Awareness of how you are not reacting.

Watch your mind . . .

Watch your thoughts and watch how quickly they can start to cultivate fear. All of which is unknown. All of which is false. In this state, your mind will make up things to fix. Things that may not need fixing. In fact, oftentimes it makes up things that will make the situation worse. You don't have to latch on to your mind's fear. Instead, observe and embrace the overwhelming sources of creation all around you. Look for ways to celebrate life and all it brings. When you do, your mind will begin to amplify joy instead of fear, and you will feel whole and complete.

Change . . .

is all there ever is and all there is going to be. To think different is an exercise in futility and frustration. The only thing that remains constant is a spirit, a muse that was here before you set foot on the ground. Your mission in life is to follow it and cast off the illusions there is something else. Embracing the present moment will project it for you. Do this and you will be rewarded. Run from it, cover it up, or ignore it, and you will feel stuck. Free yourself.

Play with Manifestation

"Expect to manifest everything
that you want to manifest."

The outside . . .

pressures don't exist. The competition is really cooperation. Your experience is not dictated for you. Your avatar does not decide. Words bend thoughts to their destination. You seek what you want to see. Keep following what works. Don't doubt what does not. Let go of all that does not help you. Don't focus on the how, focus on the why.

The unknowns . . .

around an event can lead to anxiety and fear. Your mind will want to jump into the future in an attempt to control it. Each time you do that, you will be disappointed. Instead, be grateful for all that is happening and continues to happen all around you. Release the false pressure you are putting on yourself and your environment. Then let go and allow, without focus on any thoughts of how everything is supposed to go.

Every . . .

now and then, turn around and walk the opposite direction. A whole new perspective emerges. You are in the same place, but everything is different. What was in your past is now in the future, and what you have been facing is now behind you. At any point you can change it up. You only think you can't because you have not tried it yet. We are designed to expand.

Sometimes . . .

you have the opportunity to take a leap your mind is not ready to sign off on yet. It is a natural path we all face. It can overwhelm, and it can hold you stagnant if you let it. You can overcome it by trusting the next small step. You don't have to worry about the unseen outcome down the line. All you have to focus on is the next step that brings you progress. Once taken, another one will appear for you to take, and you will be on your way. Before long you will realize you took a leap, but it did not feel like one due to the steady nature of the change.

Just because . . .

you imagine something has gone one way many times before does not mean it will go that way today. Each day there is different path to play with. Because everything changes. Your mission is to accept it. Listen without doubt or judgment to the small voice in your heart, and then take action. Your mind has no idea what is about to happen. Be at peace with that. This is freedom.

Go ahead . . .

and make plans, then release them. Follow through as you see fit, but do not hold on to any expectations of how they will go. The things that are meant to happen will, and those that aren't, will not. In any case, you have stated your intention and removed your ego from the result. Use this sense of freedom as an energy springboard. Realize you have more control than you think you do. It's a matter of perspective and resilience.

You have . . .

the option to choose how you would like to perceive your own story. You can also choose to not choose, which is a path in and of itself. The patterns are there for you to explore and to invest in. If you are often finding that choices are difficult to make, change your perception of them. See the same choices from other angles, ones where they serve you instead of block you.

Recognize...

that everyone will see their own version of reality. It comes through them from their own perceptions and visualizations. You know this because you see your own version as well. Understand it is not your place to define roles or identity for others. You cannot expect them to act the way you want them to. They have their own way of dealing with the onslaught of information and images that flood from everywhere. Instead, appreciate how they show up in your world, and let everything else go. Don't expect anything from them, and be grateful for whatever happens. For it is your own interpretation that enables the interaction at all.

Trust...

life. Trust that your body can heal. Trust that you are here for a reason. Trust that your purpose is to find out what works for you. Trust that nobody knows the answers; they just know their answer. Trust you will always have what you need. Trust you can overcome any obstacle. Trust that time is on your side. Trust that your guides are all around you. Trust that energy can enlighten and nourish. Trust that hope lives. Trust that goodness expands. Trust that everything changes. Trust that thoughts become reality. Trust that everything takes care of itself if you let it.

You can . . .

never know the causes. All is as it is because it is. To ripen under any circumstance is a matter of letting go and creating space. This starts with managing your energy. Pay attention to what drains you and remove it from your life. Be ruthless about it. Once you have done so, watch what fills the void. You will not need to do anything. You will follow your joy and follow your bliss. You will take inspired action. Because this is who you are.

Once you . . .

realize you are free, you can never go back because you have chosen to move into a place in your mind of complete acceptance. Nothing can be imposed on you because you are a witness to the events that are proceeding as they should. Nothing can be taken away from you because there is nothing to hold on to. Give up the idea of being a specific person, because your potential is so much more. You are designed to help from a place of love. All you have to do is take inspired action and be kind. You will have everything you need when you need it.

Open...

your eyes and see clearly for the first time. There is nothing to fear. All around you, chaos may reign. Let it do what it's going to do. All you can control is your direct action. Be with this and nothing else. Soon you will find that the things out of your control will fade into the background, and the things you want to see will be crystal clear and razor sharp. Then all you have to do is flow with the direction that is presented to you by your choices.

The mysteries . . .

of life are waiting for you to access. There is no manual for you to follow. There is no perfect way to proceed. Attach yourself to the way that brings you joy. Don't judge it, don't overthink it, and don't desire it. Be with it and see past it. Remove your persona from the equation and tap into the undercurrent of truth. Find what is already there.

Your internal . . .

emotions color your external world. If you live in fear, that is what you'll see. What if you do the opposite? Live in trust. Live in joy. Breathe fresh air. Allow the sun to drench you. Focus your mind on solving problems instead of predicting what might happen. Change your environment. Change your day-to-day. Change your status quo. For a couple of minutes, then hours, then days. Experiment with it. See what happens and see how it feels. You always have a choice.

Enjoy . . .

the ride. Don't take things so seriously. Even the end is just the beginning. There is nothing to be found because it is already here. All you have to do is focus on this fact over and over. Live in the flow because that is what is necessary. There is no path to take but the path that is in front of you. If you don't like the direction, pivot and go outside your mind's guidance. Then see where you end up. It may be a place you never thought of before, but one you wanted to go to. We all have blindspots, so it is important to shake the box every now and again. We are built to adapt.

Don't...

get bogged down in the *how*. If you take your focus off the how, it will appear to you. The key is to not overanalyze and stress about how something gets done. Whatever you want to do, there are always unknowns that will be present. Let go of trying to control the situation. That does not allow it to breathe. Instead focus on allowing it to happen. Once you do, watch to see what happens. Test this over and over and see what your results are. Realize you are action incarnate. Inspiration will find you, not the other way around. And you don't have to worry about all the steps, just the next one in front of you.

Thank you for reading Moving Beyond. *If you thought this book was useful, you may enjoy* Grounding from Within.

All the best.

—JMG

About the Author

Several years ago, JMG made a conscious choice to create space in his life for possibility—which continues to be a work in progress. *Moving Beyond* is his second book. You can read more of his writings at jmgbooks.com. JMG lives in Austin, TX with his wife and daughter.

www.ingramcontent.com/pod-product-compliance
Lightning Source LLC
Chambersburg PA
CBHW020543080526
44583CB00013B/974